10 Keys to Financial Freedom At An Early Age

Retire Young On A Modest Salary

Teena Smith

Copyright © 2017 Teena Smith
All rights reserved.

ISBN-13: 978-1542374514
ISBN-10: 1542374510

TABLE OF CONTENTS

Introduction 4

1. Getting Clear 7
2. Freedom Key #1: Honor God With Your Firstfruits ... 11
3. Freedom Key #2: Live Below Your Means 22
4. Freedom Key #3:
   Submit Yourself To A Strict Budget 35
5. Freedom Key #4: Set Financial Goals 43
6. Freedom Key #5:
   Master Effective Time Management 49
7. Freedom Key #6: Resist Lifestyle Inflation 59
8. Freedom Key #7: Be Grateful And Be Content 63
9. Freedom Key #8: Master Delayed Gratification 71
10. Freedom Key #9: Real Estate Is The Best Thing Since Sliced Bread 4 Winning Investment Tips 74
11. Freedom Key #10:
    A Penny Saved Is A Penny Earned 83
12. Conclusion 89

INTRODUCTION

Many imagine that achieving financial freedom at an early age is only available to those who earn large salaries over the course of their working life; or to those who inherit fortunes, win the lottery, invent things, or otherwise find themselves with large infusions of capital into their financial coffers. This couldn't be further from the truth, and I'm living proof. You see, I devoted thirty years of my life to work for modest wages, and then was able to retire at a young age and enjoy financial freedom.

I intend in this short book to share my secrets of how any person can achieve financial freedom at an early age. I will summarily lay out the steps to follow, give you some living examples, and then place it at your feet. This book has the propensity to change your life if you allow it.

If you are looking to make billions and party like a rock star, this is probably not the book for you. This book is about how to retire comfortably at an early age while earning a modest salary. It is about creating the space to have balance in your life—a relationship with God, a family, and meaningful ways to use your gifts and talents to contribute to the world.

My attention span is short. And I suspect that glorious technology has ensured that many in today's society are just like me. I am intentionally making this book short—something I intend for you to read or listen to in one sitting. I would prefer you read it, and get on with changing your life; rather than spending weeks reading or listening to the book, only to have the key messages lost in the verbosity of the text. I have personally experienced this many times. I listen to a book and get some wonderful suggestions. But then by the time I finish the book, I am overloaded with words and information. I almost feel as though I have to wade through the less important words to find the really important keys of the entire chapter.

My prayer is that this will be a book that will be listened to or read regularly. I have about ten or so such books in my audible library. Each time I listen, I hear something different—something that stands out, or answers a question in my spirit. I believe that this is the Holy Spirit. Let me explain:

Jesus promises us in John 14 that He will ask The Father to send us a Paraclete—a counselor and advocate to live inside of us, to help us and guide us.

The Holy Spirit, I believe, is that still, quiet voice in our hearts that provides answers, comfort, direction to us as we walk through life. I have learned to quiet myself, and listen for the leading of the Holy Spirit. My journal, the Bible and those ten or so books in my audible library are some of the tools that the Holy Spirit uses to guide me. For example, I wake up and talk to God about a dilemma. I talk to God mostly through my journal. I ask Him for help or guidance, or whatever. Then later, I listen to a book I may have heard 20 times, and all of a sudden the answer leaps from the text. It is something I have heard numerous times, but today the Holy Spirit uses it to provide me with a solution, or comfort, or whatever He knows I need. This is how the Holy Spirit works.

I said earlier that this book has the propensity to change your life if you let it. I believe that if you follow these steps, financial freedom will chase you. I pray that this little book will become an item in your toolbox that the Holy Spirit can use to help you.

1

GETTING CLEAR

So how does a person achieve financial freedom at a young age while earning a modest salary? Is that even possible you ask?

Well, not only is it possible, but this book will show you how. In this book, you will be given the ten keys to open the door to achieving this. The material is presented in a practical, concise manner that will help you to digest the information quickly and easily, so you can get on with implementing the steps towards financial freedom.

Now, let's talk about how to effectively use this book to change your life. Only two pieces of advice: Read it often and do what it says. So let's get started!

I want to start by dismissing a couple of misnomers. First of all, earning a large salary is not a prerequisite for achieving financial freedom. Financial freedom is available to anyone earning even a modest regular salary.

Secondly, you don't need to have special talents or higher education in order to achieve financial freedom. These are common sense steps and skills that anyone can master.

Now, let's define financial freedom. Wikipedia defines financial freedom as: *"the state of having sufficient personal wealth to live, without having to work actively for basic necessities. For financially independent people, their assets generate income that is greater than their expenses."*

I define financial freedom as:

- ➤ the freedom to travel and experience all that life has to offer without having to worry about money.

- ➤ the freedom to get up each morning and choose how I want to spend the day rather than having to show up somewhere everyday for a paycheck.

Notice that nowhere in either of those definitions is any mention of owning a palatial mansion or driving an expensive foreign car. Part of the problem is that most people associate these things with retiring and experiencing financial freedom; when quite the contrary is true. It is likely that the people you see in videos, or even in your own neighborhood who possess these "symbols" of prosperity are likely living above their means; which leads directly to financial catastrophe.

Instead, you will notice that each of these definitions of financial freedom include some inference to income being greater than expenses.

We have seen many examples in our society of profoundly rich people who earn millions of dollars each year, only to eventually end up watching their belongings being auctioned off by a court appointed bankruptcy trustee. Or professional working couples who both earn six figures, yet they are in debt up to their ears and living paycheck to paycheck. On the other hand, there are examples like me, of people who earn modest amounts and still achieve financial freedom at an early enough age to really enjoy it.

As you saw from my definition, financial freedom for me means being free to get up and decide how I want to enjoy the day -- whether I want to ride my bike on the beach, or go on a nature hike; as opposed to having to get up and get in traffic to get to a job to earn enough money to pay my bills. Financial freedom for me means

I can decide if I want to spend a month at our little beach cottage at the Atlantic Ocean or if we want to just stay at home in our little condo near the Pacific Ocean. For me, nothing about financial freedom involves mansions nor expensive foreign cars.

I want freedom, not encumbrances. I would prefer to have a small cottage on the beach that I own free and clear than a palatial mansion with a mortgage. That mortgage would require me to relinquish some of my freedom/time in exchange for work. I prefer to use my time to spend with people I love, doing things that I love.

It's okay if financial freedom looks differently for you. You may be in a position to earn significantly more than I did, and thus, be in a position to retire with bigger and better toys than me. That is absolutely fine, as long as you live by these guiding principles I will present over these next chapters.

2

FREEDOM KEY #1

HONOR GOD WITH YOUR FIRSTFRUITS

Honor the Lord with your wealth and with the firstfruits of all your produce; then your barns will be filled with plenty, and your vats will be bursting with wine.

--- Proverbs 3:9-10

King Solomon is said to be the wisest man who ever lived. We are blessed to glean wisdom from the sage advice given to his son in Proverbs 3:9-10.

King Solomon is actually giving us the formula for financial abundance. Let's look more closely at his wise counsel.

"Honor the Lord with your wealth"

You know, my husband accuses me of always trying to tell people how to do their jobs better. Well, I don't think that's true. But, if I were standing over Solomon's shoulder when he was writing this, I would have admonished him to change that verbiage to: "Honor the Lord with HIS wealth," not "your wealth." After all, it is His. We often forget that it all belongs to Him, everything, all of it. Solomon's father, King David, got it right in 1Chronicles 29:11-14 when he declares:

> *Everything in the heavens and on earth is yours, O Lord....Wealth and honor come from you alone, for you rule over everything. Power and might are in your hand, and at your discretion people are made great and given strength...But who am I, and who are my people, that we could give anything to you? Everything we have has come from you, and we give you only what you first gave us!*

So, "Honor the Lord with your wealth"; what does that really mean? I believe we can glean the answer from the Scripture we just read: "Everything we have has come from you, and we give you only what you first gave us!"

This means that we are to use the gifts and talents that God has given us to earn wealth, and then give a tithe (10%) back to God. So God first gives us the gifts and talents which we use to earn our wealth; and then we give back one tenth of that wealth, which He has first given to us.

Our wealth, our treasures are not ours. We are only stewards of the treasures he places in our charge. We are confused thinking the treasure is our own, and that we are giving God a tenth of our treasures. When actually, 100% of it belongs to Him, and He is allowing us to manage 90% of it with the charge of bringing 10% of it to His storehouse. But it gets even better. God has even made promises to us that if we are obedient to this charge that we will be blessed with abundance. We find these promises at Malachi 3:10 and Luke 6:38:

Malachi 3:10

"Bring the whole tithe into the storehouse, that there may be food in my house. Test me in this," says the Lord Almighty, "and see if I will not throw open the floodgates of heaven and pour out so much blessing that there will not be room enough to store it."

Luke 6:38

Give, and it will be given to you. A good measure, pressed down, shaken together and running over, will be poured into your lap. For with the measure you use, it will be measured to you.

God has placed finances under our stewardship. We are a fiduciary of His treasures, yet we have been given full autonomy to couple them with our talents, and to spend, invest, and manage them as we see fit for the purpose of expanding His Kingdom and territory. We know from Matthew's Gospel that Jesus laid out his expectations for us on this subject through a parable about three stewards whose master left them with this same charge, and then later returned to settle accounts with them. The one steward who had done nothing to expand his master's territory was admonished as a wicked servant. The others who had used what had been left in their care to expand the master's territory were rewarded and praised as good and faithful servants. Truly, that is the hope of every Christ follower—to earn the commendation of those six words when they stand before Christ to account: Well done good and faithful servant.

It bears noting that ten percent is only the minimum standard. Many Christians give well beyond 10%, and I can give you absolute, full assurance of one thing... you cannot out-give God. I know that may sound like a trite colloquialism, but it is incontestably true. The more you give to God, the more He gives to you in abundance.

Rick Warren, Pastor of Saddleback Church and author of "Purpose Driven Life" has this perspective on the subject of tithing:

> *"Kay and I became reverse tithers. When we got married 30 years ago, we began tithing 10%. Each year we would raise our tithe 1% to stretch our faith: 11% the first year, 12% the second year, 13% the third year. Every time I give, it breaks the grip of materialism in my life. Every time I give, it makes me more like Jesus. Every time I give, my heart grows bigger. And so now, we give away 90% and we live on 10%. That was actually the easy part, what to do with the money--just give it away, because I'm storing up treasures in heaven."*

(Honor the Lord) with the firstfruits of all your produce

Let's look at the second part of this proverb. Honor the Lord with the firstfruits of all your produce. Let's explore this term, firstfruits.

God instructed Moses to expose the secret to abundant blessing in Leviticus 23:10. He told the Israelites that when they entered the land He would give them, that they should offer a portion from their first harvest to Him. In turn, the entire crop would be blessed.

I believe that although this is not a New Testament requirement, God promises throughout Scripture to give special favor and honor to those who do make this offering. Here are some examples:

- Firstfruits givers enjoy God's comprehensive insurance. God promises that anyone who devours firstfruits givers will be held guilty and be overtaken by disaster. (Jeremiah 2:3)
- God can be called upon to give special favor to the giver of firstfruits. (Nehemiah 13)
- The giver of firstfruits offerings can expect overflowing blessings from God. (Proverbs 3:9-10)
- Giving the first portion of your financial blessing will cause all of the fruit from that blessing to be holy and multiply. (Romans 11:16)
- Giving firstfruits cause a blessing to rest upon your home. (Ezekiel 44:30)

The above Scripture gives promises of abundance and favor to those who decide to supplement their mandated 10% tithe with firstfruits offerings on each new "crop" so to speak. Some choose to do it annually with the firstfruits of their annual income. Some choose to do it when a new blessing is bestowed, for example, a new job or a new business venture. However you choose to do it, it will indeed cause your blessings to multiply in ways too numerous to count.

These countless blessings have manifested so many times in my life; I could spend this entire book telling of these supernatural events. But I will only share one such experience.

Real Life Experience

My family and I had moved to another city for a business venture that did not work out. So we decided to return to Los Angeles to the home we still owned and a job that I had arranged to begin upon our return. Long story short, we found ourselves back in Los Angeles with a job that had been delayed by three months, our house occupied by tenants who were not ready to move, and depleted savings by mechanical breakdowns while traveling across country.

We couldn't go home without paying the tenants a $20,000 relocation fee, so we were effectively homeless. I couldn't go to work for another three months, and my husband, a school teacher, had to work 30 days before a paycheck, so we were effectively unemployed. We had to take our little son and move into my friend's garage room. This was the lowest I had ever been in my life. I was so stressed that I ended up in the hospital for dehydration from my inability to keep food on my stomach.

Finally, the day came when I got my first paycheck. We were still effectively homeless. We had decided before we left Georgia that we would give my first paycheck as our firstfruits offering, but now, things were completely different than we had imagined. Notwithstanding, without a second thought, I turned the check over, signed it over to my church in Georgia, put it in an envelope and put it in the mailbox. This was a Friday.

On Saturday, we went to our postal mailbox. There we found a letter from an escrow company advising us that they had been unable to reach us, and that we needed to contact them before Monday (2 days from then) to give them our banking information so that they could wire $10,000 to us. What the heck?

You see, years earlier, a former employee had stolen $10,000 from me. I had taken this employee in and helped her buy a condo several years before that, so when she stole the money, I placed a lien on her condo. I had forgotten about it really—thought I would never see that money again. Now she was trying to sell the condo, and her escrow company was trying to pay the judgment. Moreover, when I contacted them on Monday, they advised that the calculated interest on the judgment was about $4,000, which is the amount that I had given to her as a gift for the initial down payment. God restored me completely! They sent me a bank wire for almost $14,000! Not a check, but a cash bank wire!

When we went to our postal mailbox on Monday, there was a letter from the retirement system of California, informing me that I needed to contact them to withdraw my $3,600 from their system since I no longer worked as a municipal employee. What the heck?

You see, I had worked for the City almost twenty years previously. When I left, I withdrew my 401(k) money, well at least I thought I did. Apparently, they said I left money in a small account, and now with the interest, it was $3,600. I had no idea about this! I thought I had withdrawn all my money when I left twenty years prior.

A couple of days later, we went to our postal mailbox, and there was a letter from our former mortgage company. They said we had money left in our escrow/impound account when we sold our house in Georgia, so they were refunding us over $2,000.

In all three instances, this was money that we had no idea existed. It was truly manna from Heaven. The firstfruits check I had given was less than $2,000. The manna that showed up in our mailbox was almost $20,000—ten times the seed we had sown.

And, as icing on the cake, the same Saturday that we received the $10,000 letter, we got a call from our tenants advising that they needed to break the lease and move immediately, and agreed to forfeit their security deposit. We gave them back the security deposit anyway. God had given us our home back!

There is no earthly explanation for how all five of those events lined up perfectly in the universe to occur at just the right time. The only explanation that any reasonable person could come up with is that God manipulated the resources of the universe. Think how far in advance those events had to be orchestrated.

- He knew our hearts, and knew what we would do with that first check ahead of time before I even finished earning it from work.

- The former employee who stole the money from me had to decide to sell her condo months earlier in order for escrow to be at the point of exhaustion in attempting to reach us.

- The State retirement system had to audit their books to find my forgotten account, or perhaps, there was no forgotten account, perhaps God created it for me.

- We had to forget about the impound/escrow account we had paid into the previous year when we sold our house in Georgia.

- The tenants in our Los Angeles house had to have their unexpected experience that caused their plans to change drastically, requiring them to leave immediately.

That is supernatural favor. These are the kind of unexplainable things that happen to us all the time because we give freely to God. We are so proud to say that our tithe is our largest expense, which is currently at 22% of our income. I say that not to brag, but to demonstrate how God works. Sometimes by the end of the month, I feel like the little boy with the five loaves and two little fishes. Regardless of whatever unexpected expenses may arise, we just take our tithe right off the top and keep right on paying our obligations. Money just shows up from unexpected sources at just the right time.

Anyway, as I said before, you cannot out-give God. This is only one example of supernatural, miraculous outcomes from our cheerful, generous giving to God. If you take nothing else from this book, please take this advice and give generously to God, even when it hurts.

3

FREEDOM KEY #2

LIVE BELOW YOUR MEANS

Contrary to popular belief, the key to financial freedom is not found on the Income side of your personal Profit & Loss Statement, but on the Expense side. At the end of the day, you must spend less than you earn, then save and invest what is left over. Yes, it really is that simple.

Living below your means is a life skill that must be developed regardless of how much or how little you earn. In fact, high earners are more likely to spiral out of control with their spending because earning more money tends to increase a person's sense of entitlement. The more quickly this sense of entitlement increases, the more quickly expenses related to disposable items increase. And without a budget and a clear, accurate method of tracking transactions, it won't be long before things spiral out of control and expenses exceed income, usually with the help of revolving credit.

Track Your Income and Expenses

Tracking your income and expenses is crucial. I recommend you utilize a computer and software such as QuickBooks to help you keep track of your finances. This will allow you to download your transactions directly from your bank so you can keep track of your spending throughout the month. You must set a monthly budget for yourself, and adhere strictly to that budget. We will discuss budgeting more in a later chapter.

Try to force yourself to put all of your expenditures on a debit card rather than paying cash. In fact, do your best not to use cash at all. If you do decide to use cash, you will need to do extra accounting to input each transaction manually and file the receipts in case they are needed for tax purposes.

You will need to form the habit of balancing your checkbook each month. You will be utterly surprised to find out how many bank errors, merchant overcharges, and unauthorized subscription auto-renewals you will find each month. Balancing your accounts will also allow you to catch accounting errors on your part, which are bound to happen. Perhaps the biggest benefit to balancing your accounts each month is peace of mind. You will be able to sleep easily at night knowing exactly what needs to be in which accounts to cover which expenses that might be automatically deducted. This tracking and balancing your accounts is vital. If you don't want to do it yourself, pay someone to do it for you.

Know Your Debt: Good vs. Bad

Not all debt is bad. While much of the debt people find themselves buried in is bad, there is actually such a thing as good debt. The right kind of debt is necessary as a tool in wealth-building. The right kind of debt is also necessary to establish and maintain good credit scores. Good credit scores are generated when a person demonstrates that he has a reasonable amount of good debt in relation to income, has low credit balances, and has demonstrated positive credit behavior over a long period of time. So, what is meant by "the right kind of debt" or "good debt"?

Good Debt

Good Debt is an investment in an appreciating asset or in an instrument that will generate long-term income. These instruments include mortgage loans and business loans. These instruments not only help to facilitate the acquisition of appreciating assets leading to wealth building, but they can offer tax benefits to significantly reduce tax obligations. Think of this type of debt as a tool.

Mortgage debt, in my opinion, is the best type of debt you can have. These loan products offer many benefits, including:

- Mortgage loan products help you to acquire the largest fixed assets on your balance sheet, real estate. We will discuss the magic of building a real estate portfolio later.

- Since this type of debt is secured by real estate, the lender's investment is more secure, and thus, interest rates on these types of loan products are low.

- Mortgage debt on your primary residence will allow you to deduct interest, property tax, and points. This can substantially reduce your tax obligations.

- The interest on mortgage debt on rental property can be deducted to reduce taxable rental property income.

- You can always get the cash you need by refinancing this type of loan or getting a second mortgage, though I discourage this.

- Believe it or not, it is easier to qualify for a mortgage loan than for a credit card or car. This is because it is debt secured by an appreciating fixed asset that is much more valuable than the amount of the loan. So if the borrower defaults, the lender has a greater likelihood of being able to recover his investment. Whereas, a car depreciates the moment you drive it off the lot; and thus, the debt is not reduced at the same speed that the value of the asset is reduced. So it is less likely that the lender will be able to recover his entire investment if the borrower defaults.

Bad Debt

Let's discuss bad debt. Bad Debt includes a range of consumer debt. Consumer debt is as a result of purchasing non-appreciating goods. This debt is generally used to buy disposable items—things you might find at a shopping mall. This type of debt often takes the form of credit cards, a/k/a revolving credit. The interest rates on this type of debt are generally obscenely high. Consumer debt bears a huge responsibility in enabling families to live above their means. Let's look at a couple of popular forms of consumer debt.

Credit Cards, a/k/a Revolving Credit

For the life of me, I cannot understand why this form of credit is legal. It is almost legal loan sharking. Credit card companies are allowed to extend credit at obscene interest rates. But that is not the most outrageous part of this scheme. Unsuspecting consumers are duped into accepting this credit through elaborate marketing schemes. They use popular Hollywood stars, athletes and even music celebrities to convince you that you can possess the same power, style and swag they have if you get this card in your wallet. So, you get this card, then all of a sudden you have the power to get the things you want right now, and only make small monthly payments later.

While there are many reasons why people should stay away from revolving credit, one reason stands out as the most compelling one. The way the interest and payment system is designed. This system is designed to be heavily in favor of the lender. The lender is allowed to extend credit at very high rates of interest, which is compounded daily. Then they calculate a small minimum monthly payment based on a tiny percentage of the balance and interest. Coupled together, these two factors form a system that enables the lender to hook the consumer for an extended period of time paying the amount of principal many times over before the debt is finally liquidated. Here's one example:

Let's look at a credit card with a 24.99% APR and a $2,500 balance all month. At the end of the billing cycle, the interest will be calculated as follows:

Lender calculates the Average Daily Balance (ADB) for that 31-day period. Then they calculate the Daily Periodic Rate (DPR). Then they multiply both by the number of days in the month. In this example, the

Average Daily Balance is $2,500, the DPR is .068 and the days in the month are 31. The lender then calculates the minimum payment of 1% plus interest. The statement reflects:

> Accrued interest of $52.70;
> A minimum payment of $77.70; and
> A new statement balance of $2,475.

Notice that the new statement balance is only $25 less than the previous amount due, despite the borrower having made a payment of almost $78. If this borrower continues to make the minimum monthly payments, it will take almost five years to pay off this card, and the borrower would have repaid almost double the principal amount they borrowed in the first place. So essentially, the borrower would have repaid a 100% interest rate on the principal. And no part of these calculations take into account late fees or over the limit fees that may be tacked on over the life of this loan.

The interest and payment system is one of the reasons that credit cards are such a bad idea. But there are more reasons.

> ➤ Too much of this type of debt negatively affects your credit standing. Lenders will calculate the credit limit on each card, and count that in your debt-to-income ratio. This is done even if there is no balance due on the card, because the lender feels that at any time, you can go and max out that card.

- Having balances too close to the limit on these cards indicate to a lender that you are using the credit card to balance your monthly living costs. In other words, you are living above your means, and using credit cards for regular disposable goods like grocery.

- Credit cards encourage the consumer to live above their means and hinder the development of the important life skill of delaying gratification

And for the coup de grâce, while these banks are lending this money to consumers at rates as high as 25%, they are acquiring this same money:

- From their depositors (customers) through CDs and other savings products on which they are paying 1% or 2% interest;

- From loans from other banks at interest rates as low as 0%; and

- From the federal reserve bank at rates as low as 1%.

So my advice is to stay far away from credit cards at all costs.

I hesitate to tell you, but the only way that a credit card can serve you is that it allows you to rent a car easily. So you might want to have just one that you keep active for rental car verification. But be sure to charge the actual car rental charges to your debit card, or pay it off immediately before interest rates are added.

If you have already dug yourself into this revolving credit pit, let me give you some tips to help you get to freedom sooner. Let's say you have three credit cards with balances.

- Card #1 has a $7,000 balance and an interest rate of 21%
- Card #2 has a $2,000 balance and an interest rate of 26%
- Card #3 has a $250 balance and an interest rate of 18%

You should start paying only minimum payments on Cards #1 and #3. Take every available cent you have to increase the payment on Card #2 as high as you can. The idea is that you want to quickly pay off the card with the highest interest rate first.

Once that card is paid off, move all the payments you were making over to the next highest rated card—Card #1. Dedicate all available resources to paying that card off next while only paying the minimum due on Card #3. Again, once that card is paid off, move all available funds over to Card #3. Any extra money you find should go towards paying off that revolving credit rather than to savings. Because you will only receive around 1% interest in a savings account, but pay 18% on that credit card balance.

If you find that you have dug yourself into a revolving credit hole, you may want to consider contacting a credit counseling agency. The credit counseling agency can help you develop a debt management plan. As part of this service, they will negotiate lower interest rates and payments with the creditors; then you will make one consolidated payment to the credit counseling agency. They will then disburse the funds to the various creditors.

Some of these credit counseling agencies are non-profit and can receive grants from the creditors, which help to offset their operating costs. But be very careful in choosing the right agency. Some are disreputable, and charge excessive fees or may be late paying your monthly bills, which will negatively affect your credit. A standard fee should be no more than about $50 per month. Check with the BBB or the Association of Credit Counseling Professionals before selecting an agency. Working with a credit counseling agency is not supposed to affect your FICO score negatively, but some creditors may put that information on your credit report, and it may have a negative impact on your ability to get credit. You can also attempt to negotiate a better rate or even a reduced settlement amount with each creditor yourself.

If you own a home, you might consider a second mortgage or line of credit secured by your home. This will turn that bad debt into good debt. If you do this, destroy the credit cards. <u>It is a terrible idea to make a habit of using your equity in your home to pay for disposable items purchased on credit cards. This is a one-time deal.</u> Using a loan secured by your home has a two-fold benefit. Firstly, since the loan is secured by real estate, you will be offered a substantially lower interest rate. Accordingly, your monthly payment will be substantially lower than the amount you had been paying separately to the creditors. Secondly, since this is a real estate loan, the interest is tax deductible. But please, do not make the mistake of using your equity to pay off your revolving credit, and then keep the cards. Trust me, you will eventually max those cards out again, and then you will have squandered your equity for no gain.

Auto Loans

Car loans are bad debt also, and should be avoided, if possible. These loans are bad debt because the asset being purchased is a depreciating asset. No matter how sweet the deal, the loan balance cannot keep up with the depreciation rate. Automobiles depreciate at a very high rate, starting the moment you drive it off the showroom floor.

The best way to buy a car is to decide how much of a car payment you can afford in your budget. Then each month, deposit that amount into a savings account. When you have enough in your account, buy a nice used car for cash. If you can delay your gratification and drive your old clunker for another year, you will be in a much better financial position.

If you decide that you cannot go any longer without purchasing your new vehicle with a car loan, here is some advice: It is better to buy a car that is one, preferably two years old. You can usually find cars that are being returned from a lease. Those leased vehicles are generally well cared for, have low mileage and have been kept up to date on service. Usually, a two-year-old car is still under the manufacturer's warranty. You can also sometimes find certified pre-owned vehicles in like-new condition.

Buying a two-year-old car is far better than purchasing a new vehicle, because automobiles experience their greatest depreciation in the first two years. So when you buy the two-year-old car, someone else has already taken on the burden of absorbing the depreciation. Also, the auto insurance is cheaper on a used car, and let us not forget the obvious—a used car costs less.

Also, the better your credit score, the lower interest rate you can get. Opt for the shortest term you can afford in your budget. This will save on interest.

The worst way to buy a car is through a lease. In this scenario, you basically rent the vehicle from the leasing company for a predetermined time. Your monthly payment is calculated based on the price of the car minus the projected value of the car at the end of the lease, plus acquisition fees and taxes; less any down payment. At the end of that period, you have a choice of returning the vehicle to the leasing company or purchasing the vehicle for the residual value. Upon return of the vehicle, penalties are assessed for things like high mileage or damage to the vehicle. Leasing a car is a bad idea for several reasons:

- You don't own anything. You are simply renting someone else's vehicle.

- You have no freedom. You must abide by the rules of the vehicle's owner. You can't tint your windows or install a tow hitch. You can only drive the amount of miles the owner sets forth in your lease agreement.

- You are locked in. If something arises and you are unable to make your monthly payment, you do not have the option of selling the car or returning it to the lessor without facing a steep early termination fee. If you were buying the car, you could sell it and pay off the loan. But in a lease, you would have to try to find someone qualified who might be willing to assume your lease.

At any rate, leasing is my least favorite way to acquire a vehicle .

4

FREEDOM KEY #3

SUBMIT YOURSELF TO A STRICT BUDGET

Mastering budgeting is one of the most vital things you can do in your quest for financial freedom. Simply put, a budget is a delineation of your anticipated income and expenses. There are countless benefits to mastering budgeting; here are a few:

Budgeting empowers you to tell your money where to go

Budgeting allows you to analyze your anticipated income, and strategically direct it to expenditures, savings, and investments in advance. Directing funds in this setting is much more effective than directing funds on the fly; making these decisions while standing in front of the 70" Smart TV. Doing it ahead of time removes the emotion and allows you to make more logical, sound decisions about your finances.

Budgeting allows you to keep a laser focus on your financial goals

Budgeting allows you to see how your expenditures directly affect your ultimate financial goals. A budget summarizes your expenditures, and reveals how even small, seemingly insignificant expenditures affect the bottom line. For example, on its face, stopping by to get a cup of coffee each morning before work seems insignificant. However, when it is laid out on a spreadsheet, we notice that this daily cup of jobe totals nearly $800 a year. Projected over a twenty-year period, that's nearly $16,000. How do you think that could affect your early retirement plan?

Budgeting helps you bring poor spending habits under control

The marketing experts count on us to engage in impulse spending and emotional spending. In fact, they entice us to it, manipulate us to it even. Through strategic marketing, they:

> ➤ Demonstrate that we need their products and merchandise in order to be sexy, smart, fabulous; or

- ➢ Convince us that if we use their products, our workload will be greatly reduced—dirt will just fall off, children will want to do their chores for the opportunity to use these wonderful products; or

- ➢ Convince us that we need their products in order to be a good mother or a responsible pet owner.

Budgeting helps us gain control over these marketing tactics. Our spending is more planned and managed. When we go to a store with a planned amount that we can spend, it sets the stage for strength to combat these urges.

Budgeting helps you to master delaying gratification

Delaying gratification is another vital tool in achieving financial freedom. Delaying gratification is the ability to resist the temptation for an immediate reward in lieu of a later, more lasting reward. This is a skill that will be required to achieve financial freedom. Delaying gratification is required to drive an old clunker for another year in order to save the cash to pay for your next car without an auto loan.

Budgeting helps to achieve peace of mind knowing you are prepared for emergencies

Knowing that you can meet your obligations and that you have money in a savings account will allow you to rest at night. Peace of mind automatically accompanies the knowing that you will be able to buy a plane ticket home on short notice in case of an emergency, or knowing that an unexpected auto repair will not affect your ability to meet your monthly obligations. Budgeting can help you to create this for yourself.

Setting Up A Winning Budget

Of course there are many ways to set up a budget, but the following budget is one that I recommend, and one that God will bless. It is based on the principle of living on no more than 70% of your income, and saving and investing the balance. I call this the 70/10/10/10 budget. Here are the components:

10% The first 10% always goes back to God

10% After God, always pay yourself next (savings)

10% Invest

70% Leftover to budget frugally for living expenses

Pay God First

Remember, Chronicles 29:11-12 tells us that everything in heaven and on the earth is God's. We are stewards of his treasures. At least the first 10% should always be reinvested back into the Kingdom. We elaborated on this in an earlier chapter.

Pay Yourself Next

We make a habit of paying our creditors regularly. We have to think of our savings as an obligation that we must meet. By doing this, we assign importance to it—we make it clear that this is a priority in our lives. Having savings money in the bank creates security and prepares us for unforeseeable obstacles or for opportunities that may present themselves.

Again, 10% is the minimum. The more you can save, the better. For many years, by living below my means, I was able to live on one of my semi-monthly paychecks and save the other. I saved 50% of my earnings. This allowed me to be in a position to take advantage of cash real estate deals that came along.

How I Was Able to Live on 50% Of My Income

As I mentioned in an earlier section, when I left my tenure with the City, I withdrew the $20,000 that was vested in my retirement plan. To avoid penalties for early withdrawal, I used it to put down on a condo. I purchased a 1-BR condo for $70,000. With the $20,000 down payment, my mortgage was less than $500 per month. I was driving an older car that was already paid off. I lived alone, so my utilities were minimal and so was my grocery bill. Each time I got a pay increase, I increased my savings deposits, not my expenses. This enabled me to be able to pay all my expenses from one paycheck. Then I saved the second paycheck.

Invest In The Future

You should be contributing 10% of your salary to some type of long-term growth vehicle such as a 401(k), a whole life insurance policy, a 529 Plan if you have children, etc... The earlier you start, the better. Choose a financial planning expert with whom to work. Choose carefully. Do your research and check their references.

The Remaining 70%

Properly allocating the 30% does not give you a free pass to squander the remaining 70%. Remember, even the 70% belongs to God. That's why good stewardship should be a priority. Adhering to a strict budget will help you in this process.

Here are a few budgeting tips:

- Estimate your fluctuating expenses such as utility bills on the high side.

  At the end of the month, any remaining funds in that line item should be transferred to savings. So if you have budgeted $50 for electricity, but your bill is only $32, the $18 should be transferred to savings.

- Always balance your checkbooks.

  Accounting software such as QuickBooks is very helpful in keeping track of your finances.

- Remember, the goal is to spend less than you earn. Live below your means.

On the next page, you will find a breakdown of the budget components.

10 Keys to Financial Freedom At An Early Age

Sample Budget

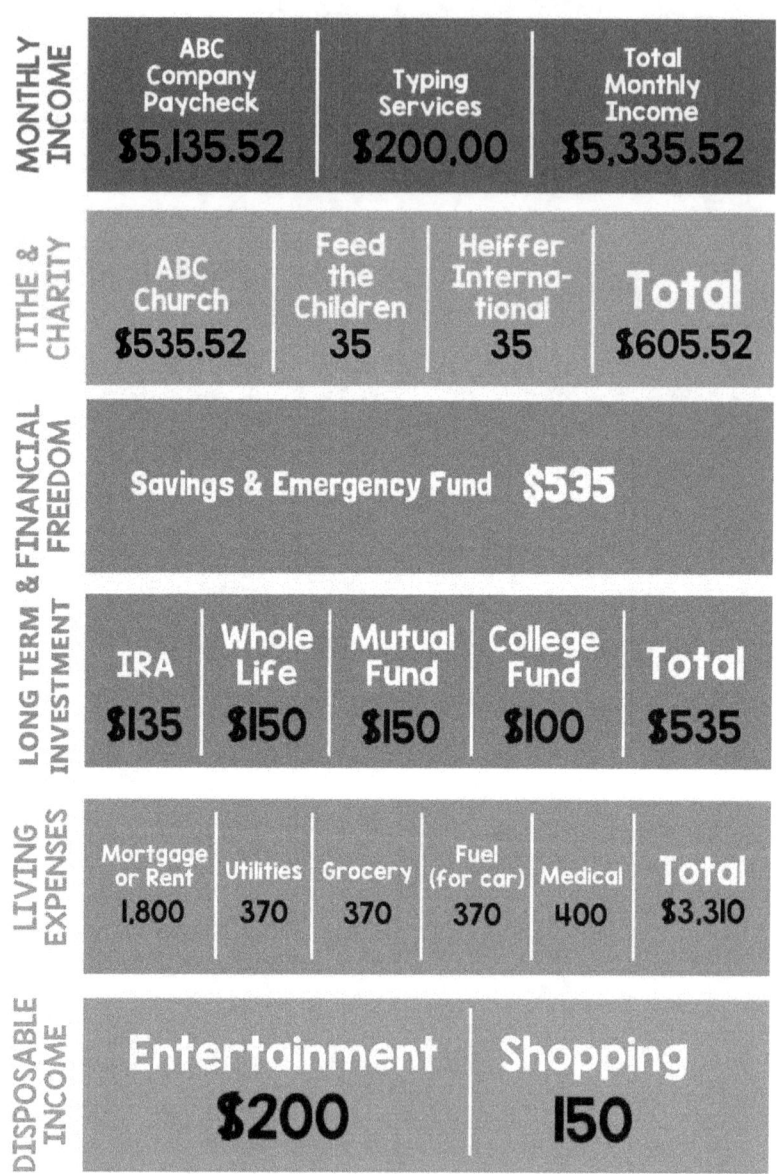

5

FREEDOM KEY #4
SET FINANCIAL GOALS

Goal setting is truly one of the most important life skills that you will need to master. Goal setting helps you to set the direction for your life. In my opinion, Brian Tracy is The Master of this subject. I highly recommend you read some of his books on the subject of goal setting. Brian Tracy suggests that you would never get into your car and just start driving without having a destination. But rather, you decide where you are going, and map out your route either in your head or on your smart device. He goes further to suggest that setting a goal is like programming a heat-seeking missile. It will seek out, move and track your goal relentlessly.

There are guidelines to developing effective goals.

- First of all, you have to decide exactly what it is that you want to achieve.

- Next, you have to identify all of the steps that will be required to achieve this goal. What habits, skills, knowledge, contacts will you need to develop?

- Next, you will need to clearly write out your goals in detail. This detail must include timelines and benchmarks.

- They should be written in positive, present tense language as though the goal had already been achieved. For example, "I am living within my means and using only money available to me that is already in the bank via my debit card" as opposed to, "I am not using revolving credit anymore."

- As soon as a goal is written, then action should be taken immediately – some action that moves you forward towards achieving that goal. Every single day something should be done to move you closer to that goal.

> The goal(s) should be posted in a prominent place and reviewed often. Your goals become your "why" and motivate you to engage in delayed gratification.

> Don't share your goals with anyone who might possibly discourage you or offer you well-meaning, negative advice.

Cultivate your garden. Although this is not directly related to goal-setting, it is very useful in keeping you on track with your goal achievement. So what exactly does "cultivate your garden" mean? Another of my favorite authors, Wayne Dyer adapted this from Voltaire's Candide, pointing out that as a gardener, he learned that weeds automatically grew in his garden. No matter what he did, he could not get rid of them. He tried pulling them, using chemicals to kill them, even burning them, and they always returned. He said the only way he found to eliminate the weeds was to grow something else to choke out the weeds. In the same way, the idle mind left on its own will grow weeds naturally. He suggests that we must plant something positive by reading books, listening to lectures and sermons, taking classes, growing and developing in some way. So I pass along this wise counsel to you. Cultivate your garden.

Any goals, but especially financial goals, should be developed, monitored and revised with input and direction from God; since it is His treasure and you are only the steward. I strongly recommend annual God retreats, and regular consultation with God in this area.

As an executive in an organization, we had annual staff retreats. We would go to a nice hotel for a week and have meetings that included brainstorming sessions. We would review our existing mission statement, and over the week's time, develop a new strategic plan for the organization. This plan would set the direction for the organization for the coming year that was in line with the ultimate mission. It would include measurable goals and benchmarks.

I adopted this model for my personal goals. Each year, I have a daylong God retreat at the ocean—I personally find God where the ocean meets the land. Together we review my past year's goals and follow the same format to develop new annual goals, monthly goals, and sometimes daily goals. I leave these sessions with clearly written out goals with timelines and benchmarks. Halfway through the year, I have a half-day retreat to review my progress to make sure I am on track. This is how my personal financial goals have looked over the years:

> My long term financial goal since I started working has been to retire by age 40.

> I had annual financial goals that supported that plan, to include paying off properties to create residual income and sacrificing to contribute to other long term strategies while in my 20s and 30s.

> I had monthly financial goals that included strategies to meet those annual and long-term goals such as keeping living costs below my means, and not driving a new car every year. These goals were tracked closely with monthly budgeting.

Stephen Covey says we should begin with the end in mind. That advice could not be more relevant to setting financial goals. Keep in mind that you will need to develop several sets of goals.

You should have your long-term financial goals; that is to say, goals that are related to your purpose or your "end game"—how you want to end up. You need to have annual financial goals. These goals are ones that are set each year after your annual spiritual retreat, which I discussed earlier in this chapter. Your monthly financial goals are best expressed in the form of a monthly operating budget. Your weekly and daily goals should be reflected as line items on your "to do" list. You see, the weekly and daily goals are basically time management tools. I would be remiss if I did not spend some time on the very important life skill of time management.

In the next chapter, you will find a diagram of Stephen Covey's four quadrant system.

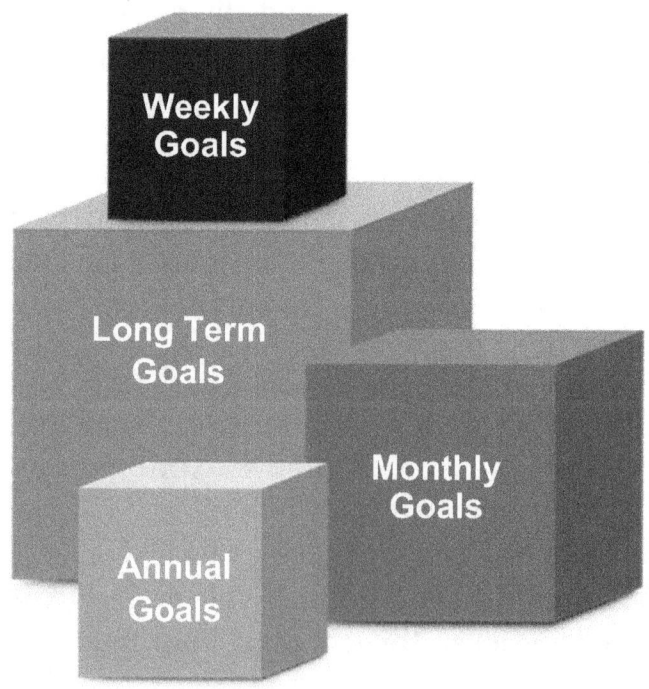

6

FREEDOM KEY #5

MASTER EFFECTIVE TIME MANAGEMENT

*E*ffective time management is one of the most important life skills to master. So why is this so important you ask?

Here's the thing: Each of us experiencing this life cycle gets 24 hours in each day. There is absolutely nothing we can do to get more hours. Time is valuable and limited.

When we effectively manage our amount of allotted time, we get more important work done in a shorter amount of time, which in turn, creates more time for us to build superior human relationships and work towards self-actualization.

Let's start by first defining time management. The business dictionary defines time management as the systematic, priority-based structuring of time allocation and distribution among competing demands. In layman's terms, time management is deciding in advance the most efficient way to spend an allotted amount of time.

We discussed budgeting in an earlier chapter, and how it empowers us to decide in advance and to direct our money where to go. Similarly, time management is like budgeting our time – deciding in advance how and where it should be spent. We often recognize the value of our currency, but often forget the value of our precious, limited time.

I want to offer you just a few strategies that might assist you in your quest to mastering time management.

    a. Do the most important tasks first. Brian Tracy has written an entire book dedicated exclusively to this strategy called, "Eat That Frog." Using the analogy of the most important task being a big nasty frog, Tracy suggests that you should eat that first. Then, he suggests, the remaining tasks will seem effortless.

The third of Stephen Covey's 7 Habits of Highly Effective People is "Put First Things First." Covey places such a high value on this habit that he developed an elaborate time management tool in the form of a 4-quadrant "to do" list, which we will delve more deeply into later in this chapter.

b. You must become proficient at the art of saying, "no". Remember, time is precious and limited. You have decided what it is you are working towards, and you have set goals accordingly. You have planned your day in advance. Now you must guard your time and commitment to your goals carefully. You must learn to say no even to tasks that may be worthwhile or fun, or even those into which you may have been guilted.

Pray for wisdom and discernment in this area. From time-to-time an opportunity may fall into your lap that was not previously scheduled on your list, but it clearly enriches you in some positive way that moves you closer to your dreams. Perhaps an opportunity to train or learn a new skill comes along, or an opportunity to work with a potential mentor materializes.

Some time ago, I asked my Pastor to sit on a board of an important ministry. She asked for time to pray about it, then got back to me with the most sincere and eloquent "no" I think I have ever heard. Truly though, I learned from her that day.

She didn't try to make excuses, she didn't try to explain why her ministries were more important, she simply told me the truth. She said in effect that while that work sounded like important work for God, she was very busy doing the work to which God has called her. And taking on another commitment would distract her and cause her God-work to suffer. And ultimately, she must be obedient to God's call on her life.

So, now let's practice it together……just say "no".

c. Trim the fat. That's my way of saying, get rid of some of the fluff, or at least strategically work it into your schedule. By fluff, I mean time wasters like junk TV, surfing the web, or video gaming. Things that eat up your time and in exchange, offer nothing of substance to enhance your life. You can find ways to add some of this fluff back into your life by strategically coupling them with quality activities. For example, I record all my junk TV programs, and only allow myself to watch them while I am at the gym on a cardio machine. I am so into the show that it completely distracts me from how tired I am, and before I realize it, sweat is pouring off of me. I have even had times when I went to the gym a second time in the evening because I wanted to see the season finale of a series.

d. Honor your vessel. Create time in your daily schedule to enhance and preserve your physical, emotional and spiritual health.

Physical Health

On the physical side:

a. Do at least 20 minutes of cardio exercise at least 4 times a week;

b. Eat sensibly and in moderation.

c. Drink plenty of water.

d. Get enough sleep. This is your body's chance to heal and rejuvenate. Try to get 7 to 8 hours of sleep each night.

Emotional Health

To strengthen emotional health:

a. Cultivate your garden. We discussed that at length in a previous chapter. You must be proactive in keeping your mind focused on positive growth. Read and listen to books, take classes, keep growing and your emotional health will hold you up.

b. Don't be afraid of counseling or therapy, or a life coach even. Sometimes, we are just too close to a situation to recognize a pattern, or spot an easy solution. Sometimes an unbiased third party can quickly mediate a dysfunction or dispute between two people that could completely transform the relationship. Sadly, some people foolishly leave this valuable tool out of their toolboxes.

Spiritual Health
Maintain your spiritual health by:

a. Going to bed early and rising early; then

b. Spending some alone time talking with Your Maker each morning before you get going. I believe we are most receptive to the leading of The Holy Spirit early in the morning. Throughout the Bible, God had the really important conversations with people early in the morning while the dew was still on the rose.

Stephen Covey's Time Management Matrix

As mentioned earlier, Stephen Covey developed a time management tool based on an unmet need that he perceived existed. Covey's premise is that there will always be multiple tasks that overlap and compete for our attention; and without a system, we will tend to respond to tasks based on their urgency without taking into consideration their importance. To address this, Covey developed a system that requires you to first sort the task into one of four sections entitled, "Urgent, Important" "Not Urgent, Important" "Urgent, Not Important" and "Not Urgent, Not Important". To do list items are sorted by importance within the quadrants; then he suggests working from the quadrants. The urgent and important tasks must be dealt with immediately.

Without question, tasks in Quadrant 1 must be dealt with first. Quadrant 2 contains tasks that are not urgent but important. These tasks could be categorized as more preventive or preparatory in nature. They are generally tasks that require you to prioritize and schedule them on your own, as these tasks don't "notify" you of their urgency like a ringing phone or other Quadrant 3 tasks. Tasks that you might find in Quadrant 2 include tasks and activities such as balancing your bank account or spending quality time with your spouse or children. Covey surmises that most of our time should be spent working on Quadrant 2 tasks and activities. For these items are certainly important; but they are not clambering for our immediate attention, like a ringing phone. Covey purports that when we are not handling the items in Quadrant 2, they will automatically get pushed into Quadrant 1.

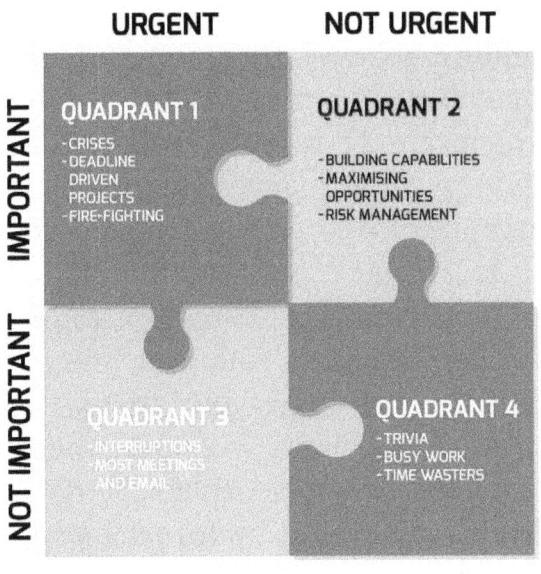

Quadrant 1 contains tasks that are urgent and important. Tasks in this Quadrant tend to be critical in nature. These tasks generally have serious consequences, strict deadlines or could have a significant impact if shirked.

Following Covey's logic of Quadrant 2 items shifting to Quadrant 1 automatically, if the bank account in the first example was not balanced as a Quadrant 2 task, serious consequences might result – the account could overdraw. All of a sudden, you are thrust into Quadrant 1 tasks such as driving around to vendors and employees trying to restore right relations and replace the bad checks. Following the second example, if you failed to prioritize your spouse and carve out time for them as a Quadrant 2 task, then you might be deeply impacted by your spouse's decision to divorce you. Again, you would be thrust into Quadrant 1 tasks such as attending mediation hearings and restorative counseling sessions to try to save your marriage.

Quadrant 3 tasks are the most clever thief of your time. Tasks in this quadrant are urgent but not important. Quadrant 3 tasks generally have some type of "notification" system attached to them that disrupts everything and demands your immediate attention; yet they are not necessarily tasks that are important. Quadrant 3 tasks may include a chime alerting you to new email while working on a deadline. It may include an unannounced visit from your gossipy coworker or even a ringing phone during dinner with your family.

These disruptions are "in your face" demanding to be addressed immediately.

Highly effective people set aside specific blocks of time to deal with Quadrant 3 tasks. They generally have outgoing messages on their communication devices or auto reply messages on their emails advising that they are working on deadlines and will return calls, emails, etc... during several predetermined times they have blocked off in their schedule. Then they respond or sort these tasks all at once during these blocks of time.

When they are disrupted by gossipy coworkers, they kindly and firmly let them know that they are working on a critical deadline and must get back to work. If they are the really persistent type that won't leave on their own, another strategy is to get up, put your hand on their shoulder, and while listening, walk them back to their desk, and then politely excuse yourself.

Quadrant 4 tasks are not urgent and not important. Tasks and activities in this Quadrant are more recreational in nature. These activities don't generally contain profound inherent enriching qualities on their own. I mean, sure we all need "down-time" and these activities generally serve us well during those times. Some activities that might be found in this Quadrant include spending time on Facebook or other social media sites; talking on the phone about negative, gossipy or unproductive topics; or watching junk TV.

As I mentioned in a previous chapter, some of these Quadrant 4 activities could be made crucial by coupling them with other more important, less fun activities. For example, as I mentioned earlier, I record all my junk TV series, and only allow myself the "treat" of watching them when I am on a machine at the gym. Otherwise, I can't watch them. In this way, this otherwise useless, unproductive activity becomes a valuable tool in my quest to maintain my physical and emotional health through daily exercise. I mean, I don't hate exercise, but I certainly would not be chomping at the bit to get to the gym every day if I weren't dying to see the season finale of the 250th season of "Grey's Anatomy" or some other foolishness I am hooked on.

7

FREEDOM KEY #6
RESIST LIFESTYLE INFLATION

Lifestyle inflation refers to the practice of increasing your expenses when your income increases. Generally, each year you will receive pay increases due to COLA (cost of living adjustments), promotions or merit increases, or even bonuses. If you were engaged in lifestyle inflation, you would increase your expenditures to match the increase in your income. It's almost an unspoken thought…"oh, I can afford that now"—a low-pitched sense of entitlement that creeps in to almost subliminally influence your spending decisions. Almost without realizing it, you add a small monthly expense here or there; you hold your budget reigns a little less tightly, and before you know it, your lifestyle has elevated.

Let's examine an example up close.

You are called into your boss' office and learn that you are being promoted to "senior" something or the other. Along with this promotion, you will be receiving a 25% increase in your pay. This increase will be reflected in your next paycheck.

It nearly escapes your notice that over the next few months, you have slowly increased your monthly expenditures, and you now find yourself floating to the end of each paycheck, just as you had before your raise. You sit down to analyze how you have met with this outcome. You look at the changes in your lifestyle since the raise:

You traded in your car and got a new one which increased your car payment from $300 to $600 per month and you subscribed to satellite radio in your new car for $15 per month. According to your calculations, you should have still seen an increase in your monthly income because your pay increased by 25% or $400 per month, and you only spent $315 of that raise. However, your calculations did not factor in a few very important things.

First of all, you had estimated an increase in your biweekly paycheck of $200, after all that is a 25% increase from your former paycheck. However, you did not take into account the increase in the withholding based on the larger gross amount. So your increase was only $150.

Another problem is that you did not realize that the more expensive car caused an increase in your car insurance by $20 per month. So you actually increased your monthly expenses by $335, while your pay has only increased by $300 per month. Additionally, the increase could push you into a higher tax bracket, and thus you could experience a higher income tax rate at the end of the year, which would increase your tax liability.

Here is the prudent way that increases of any kind should be handled. Firstly, you should wait until the recalculations are done and you receive you first paycheck reflecting a full pay period at the increased rate. During this waiting period, nothing should change. No expenditures should be made and any partial increases should be saved.

Once you receive the full paycheck, then you can sit to revise your monthly budget. The increase should be divided into thirds, and allocated to the line items for your tithe, your savings and your investment accounts. All other line items should remain the same.

If there are any bad debt items looming overhead, then the amount being allocated to savings and investment should be temporarily directed to that bad debt to help retire it more quickly. Once the bad debt is liquidated, then those funds should be redirected back to savings and investment. The regular budget line items should remain the same with no increases, unless of course, it is a true cost of living increase such as property taxes, utility bills, etc...

This is sometimes difficult to do. Often, along with a promotion comes an attitude of entitlement. A perception that since I am a "senior" something or the other, I should live in a bigger place or drive a nicer car. We have to resist this entitlement attitude and stand strong in our commitment to delaying our gratification. After all, we are working toward a goal of early retirement.

8

FREEDOM KEY #7

BE GRATEFUL AND BE CONTENT

These two concepts are interconnected and directly affect each other. Maintaining an attitude of gratitude creates contentment. Practicing the art of being content with what you have leads to gratitude. And it follows that learning to master the art of being content leads directly to happiness.

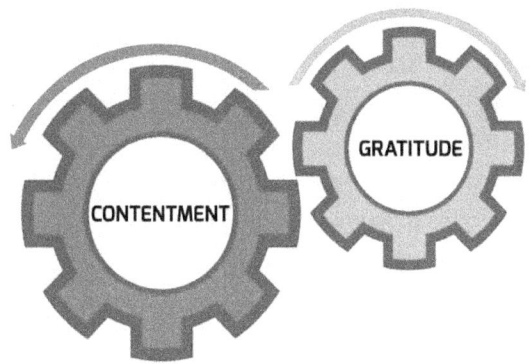

You can't practice either one of these without affecting the other, either positively or negatively. If you never learn to be content with what you have, it will lead to ingratitude; and inversely, if you are ungrateful, it will lead to your lack of contentment.

I believe the problem starts with coveting. Coveting is certainly not a new concept. It was obviously an issue in early biblical times, as God felt it worth including as one of the ten laws He gave to Moses to pass down to the Israelites.

Covetousness found its way throughout the ages, and in the more recent past, its reaches were limited to small circles. A neighbor covets the new car in his neighbor's driveway; or a sibling covets his brother's new home. The neighbor who covets his neighbor's new car is shifting his energy from the gratitude for his own blessing of a car in his own driveway. He does not realize that the car in his neighbor's driveway is heavily financed with a sizeable car payment. His car, modest it may be, is paid off and he holds his own title free and clear. Similarly, his brother's brand new house comes with a hefty mortgage payment and homeowners association dues while his small house is paid in full.

While coveting is always dangerous, when encountered only occasionally and in close-knit circles, it is generally easier to manage. It often involves people who love each other - sometimes siblings, or close friends. They can talk and share honestly about both the benefits and the burdens associated with the coveted item; and their intentions are not generally to make the other feel badly or rub their blessing in the other's face.

But today's technology has created a huge platform, a fertile ground upon which covetousness can thrive and spread like wildfire. Thanks to social media, we are bombarded with images and information instantly 24 hours a day, 7 days a week.

Social media is a platform that delivers instant coveting opportunities to any handheld device in milliseconds. These coveting opportunities can come in any form, big or small, many times each hour of the day, depending on how many friends we follow on Instagram, Facebook, Twitter, Snapchat, or any of the many other instant sharing mediums. And these broadcasts are not seasoned with love and caring consideration not to rub success in the face of the other person, like one may encounter in small social settings like described earlier.

You can see the new red bottom shoes your friend purchased before she leaves the checkout counter. You see the flowers your friend's husband sent her just because; or see the new sportscar your friend just purchased before he even drives it off the showroom floor. You can even witness the blessing of a newborn baby whose umbilical cord has just been cut.

Social media is nothing more than a huge platform on which people can sell you these fantasies of how perfect their dream lives are. The problem is that they only show you the good, amazing, happy things about their lives. Using the same examples from above:

- The friend who posts her new red bottom shoes does not mention that she didn't have the $1,500 in the bank for them, so she purchased them on a credit card with a 23% interest rate. And from our earlier discussion on revolving credit compound interest, we know she will be paying for those shoes 5 years from now.

- The friend whose husband sent her flowers just because doesn't share that her husband has anger management issues, and sent her flowers as an apology for berating her before she left for work.

- The friend who posted the car from the showroom floor does not mention that he is only leasing this car, and he does not even own a home or have a garage to park it in.

- And the beautiful blessing of a newborn child, which is the most intimate moment a couple should be sharing with God, is shared with the world, including the struggling childless person.

These instant communication tools really challenge us in our quest to practice the art of contentment. It is easy to buy into the fantasy being sold over social media. When we see what looks like the perfect "whatever," then our blessing of grapes turn sour in our mouth. All of a sudden, ours doesn't taste as sweet. The seed of discontentment has been planted. That is the danger of coveting. Coveting blinds us to our blessings.

When the friend posts the flowers her husband sent her just because you started to belittle your own husband in your mind because he has never sent you flowers just because. You forget the qualities with which your own man is endowed. Your husband is a man rooted firmly in his relationship with God. He is a good husband and father and a provider for your family. And he cooks! But now, he doesn't buy you flowers, but he also doesn't verbally abuse you like your friend's husband does.

The instant we catch ourselves engaging in covetousness at any level, we must immediately stop and refocus our attention on our own blessings. A good exercise to do in these instances is to make a list of every blessing you can think of.

I get it, coveting makes contentment more challenging, yet, it is vital that we master this art of being content with what we have. The only way that we will be able to master this is to come to the understanding that God created each person uniquely, with their own talents and abilities; and He set forth work, experiences, opportunities and people that are unique to that individual's journey. So each of us must take the talents and gifts that have been given to us, and run the race marked out for us. We must understand that what God has placed on another's path is for them, and not for us. We must remember that God is our Father. We must be assured that He loves us and will provide us with everything that we need, but not necessarily everything we want. I mean, would a good father give his child only candy to eat because the child wants it, when the father knows he needs vegetables, fruit, and protein? Of course not. But does this mean that father does not love that child? Absolutely not. In fact, it demonstrates how much that father does love that child.

Only once we come to that realization will we be able to truly practice contentment with what we have. Then gratitude will follow easily; and vice versa. It is easy to see how blessed we are when we just stop and notice. Try it with me now.

Notice how your breath goes in and out, and your heart is beating rhythmically. This means that your respiratory and circulatory systems are working perfectly. Notice the black words on this white page. This means you have been blessed with the gift of vision and mental wellness. You get the idea? And what about our lifestyle? Unlike many around the globe, we have our primary needs met—food, basic shelter, and clothing to protect us from the elements.

We must get in the daily habit of quieting ourselves, listing and being grateful for our blessings before we start each day. This will help us to develop our attitude of gratitude.

As if we needed a commandment, the Bible has almost 25 instances where we are told to be grateful and to thank God, Our Heavenly Father. As a parent, my son, who is one of the most grateful people I know, motivates me to want to do more for him than he will even accept. In the same way, I imagine that my extreme gratitude has some bearing on how my Heavenly Father showers me with favor and blessings.

If you could believe it, there are other benefits to gratitude besides God's blessings. There are actually scientifically proven physical, mental and emotional health benefits. Gratitude improves sleep, increases mental and physical energy, reduces stress, improves self-esteem, helps with depression and improves overall happiness.

Mastering this cycle of contentment and gratitude increases our opportunities to build our wealth because we are less likely to engage in coveting behaviors of trying to "keep up with the Jones'." We are more likely to be genuinely happy when we see others prosper or have good fortune. This is because we know that what they have received is what God has set aside for them. We know from Scripture that everything in heaven and on earth belongs to God. There is plenty. Because God blessed another person does not mean that there is less blessing left available for me. There is enough for everyone.

Mastering contentment and gratitude helps to keep us focused on running our own race; and so we are more likely to be more disciplined with staying focused on our goals, particularly our financial goals.

9

FREEDOM KEY #8

MASTER DELAYED GRATIFICATION

We've touched on this concept in previous chapters, but basically, delayed gratification is the ability to resist the impulse to take an immediately available reward, in the hopes of obtaining a more valued reward in the future. The problem is that most people never learn this vitally important life skill.

We live in a microwave society. People are used to getting things right now. These large retailers work together with large financial conglomerates to develop elaborate marketing schemes aimed at convincing consumers that they cannot live without their products; and moreover, that they don't have to wait, they can get it now for a small monthly payment. And so, we never learn to control our impulses and desires. So our income can never keep up with our impulses. So we can never get to the place where we are earning more than we are spending.

It's easier to make a sacrifice if we know our sacrifice has a purpose. So we again rely on Stephen Covey's advice, and begin with the end in mind. The writer of Hebrews opens his 12th chapter by admonishing us to run with perseverance the race marked out for us with our eyes fixed on Jesus, who gave us the best example of delayed gratification known to man. The writer tells us that Jesus practiced this by looking ahead to the joy of seating himself at the right hand of God, The Father, and because of that, was able to endure the cross.

When we follow this sage advice, we can follow Jesus' example of fixing our eyes on the end of the race—the goal. Just like a camera lens, when we focus on one thing, all the other surrounding things become blurred. When we are successful in this, it becomes easier for us to make wise financial choices. We see that new pair of shoes, or new car as blurred objects, and see the goal of retiring early with perfect clarity.

10

FREEDOM KEY #9

REAL ESTATE IS THE BEST THING SINCE SLICED BREAD
4 WINNING INVESTMENT TIPS

I have found no better wealth building vehicle than real estate. It has been a tremendous blessing to me. Real estate investing is such a vast industry with many ways to capitalize off of its opportunities.

While there are many ways to make tremendous profits, I guess in the end it just comes down to personal goals. For me, when I set out with my early retirement plan, I knew that I only wanted to work a certain number of years, long enough to pay off properties that I had strategically acquired in anticipation of residual income for my retirement. My attitude all along has been, "I don't need a mansion on the beach; a cottage on the beach that is paid off is good for me." I just believe that in order to have the mansion, it will require some costs I have not been willing to pay. Let me explain:

In order to make billions in real estate, I would have had to take bigger risks in order to make bigger profits. I chose a safer path of investing in smaller, less expensive properties that would generate steady income. I always chose properties that I could afford to make the mortgage payment on if it were vacant for a few months, as is the nature of rental properties. Had I invested in more expensive properties, during those times, I might have lost everything.

I knew that making larger, more risky investments would require more of my time—I would have to devote more of my life into that venture. I wanted to have a family and to have space in my life to be a mom. I didn't want to get to my retirement and then have to spend it alone. As I said before, I guess it just comes down to what you ultimately want.

As I said previously, if you choose to retire with bigger and better toys than me, that is absolutely fine, and quite possible as long as you turn these 10 Keys to habits, and incorporate them into your master plan.

Let me take some time and share the success strategies that have worked for me; and to offer you some sage advice.

Include God

Firstly, I would never even venture to set my long term goals without consulting with My Creator. If someone creates a computer, the computer doesn't know everything it is capable of. Only the creator knows. He can develop a manual to explain all the functions, but ultimately, He is the only one who knows exactly what the computer is designed to do. In the same way, God created me, so he knows exactly what I am designed to do. If I want to cooperate with The Spirit and with the universe, I will have easier success if I get my direction from My Creator—The Source.

Some experts say that Michael Phelps' body was designed to swim. Well, supposed he decided that he instead wanted to be a gymnast. I'm sure with his determination, he could pull it off and perhaps be good at it. But by cooperating with The Spirit and becoming a swimmer, his success is much easier and much greater. Similarly, if God designed and gifted you to be a world-renowned worship leader, and you instead followed in your parent's steps and took over the accounting firm, having to wear a black or blue suit with a white shirt and tie every day, you could be successful, but you would likely be miserable, sitting at a desk counting beans every day. You may one day strangle yourself with your necktie.

My point is, consult with God about what your ultimate goals should be. This can only be done in quiet time with Him. Sitting with pen and paper in hand, feeling, groping even for His leading. I find a better connection with God when I go into nature, either a beach or a park surrounded by trees, or even a grassy knoll.

Step 1: Decide in what type of property you will invest

To do this effectively, you have to first decide on what type of tenant you want and what you are willing to pay to get it. My first decision was that I did not want to invest in single family structures (stand-alone houses), because there are too many things that can easily fall into disrepair. I wanted something with less maintenance, less breakable things.

I did not want a multi-family dwelling (apartment building) because generally speaking, the type of person who rents an apartment is different than the person who primarily rents condos. This is due partly because in a condo complex, there are generally more rules, and many of the neighbors are owners operating with pride of ownership. They are more likely to complain and cause problems for people who disregard the rules. Generally, the person who is willing to live in that setting is a person who wants to follow the rules anyway; generally, a more mature renter who cares more about the environment. I wanted the type of tenants who pay their rent by depositing it into my bank account. I didn't want the type of tenant from whom I would have to go and collect their rent.

Now, the cost of having this type of renter is that the net proceeds will be less because of HOA dues within a condo complex. In the end, you have to decide what you are willing to live with. For me, I wanted my real estate rentals to be passive income that would not interfere with my parenting or with my daytime job. So I was willing to take a little less monthly in exchange for the peace of mind that comes along with the latter.

Step 2: Start Small

I started my real estate ventures by purchasing a small condo in an area where I both liked and felt was a good rental market. Although I could have afforded a bigger place, I just wanted something small that would be easy to rent out later. Also, I wanted a small mortgage.

Remember, this is not your dream home; you are not buying this as the final place you will live. Instead, focus on the rentability of the property. Choose location over size. In the end, property values will hold more steadily in a good market, even if the place is smaller.

Choose something with a small enough mortgage payment that you could easily afford to make the mortgage payment from your paycheck for at least 3 months. Having vacancies is part of the rental business. You must have a small fund available for repairs, emergencies or vacancies.

Remember, real estate is an appreciating asset. This is especially true in good markets. So don't be concerned about buying an inexpensive property. I bought a $64,000 property in 1984, and sold it in 2006 for $410,000. Not only did I enjoy a 641% Return On Investment, but over the course of the 22 years I owned the property, I got other benefits including:

> A. I received net income each month (Rental Income less Mortgage, Taxes, Insurance);

> B. I received the tax write-off that allowed me to reduce my taxable income;

> C. This asset allowed me to refinance several times whenever I needed cash.

Step 3: Diversify

Diversification is always a good thing, but especially true in real estate investing. This is another reason I never liked investing in multi-family dwellings (apartment buildings.) Too much of your money is tied up in this one investment. If, by chance, this investment turns out to be the Titanic, then your entire portfolio does not go down with it.

You should expect that there will be at least one bad investment in the life of your real estate career. My one occurred when I decided to go down to Gulfport, Mississippi after Hurricane Katrina to take advantage of some "fire sale" I thought. I was banking on the market recovering, and me being able to enjoy some quick-found equity. I had done my market research even before Katrina, and had discovered that Mississippi had the lowest property values of any oceanfront state. Although Biloxi had been revitalized, Gulfport was still underdeveloped. I thought that this was a sleeper—that Gulfport had to be on the cusp of revitalization.

Instead, what actually happened is that the economy was just so bad there, even before Katrina. There were no major employers, and many were well below the poverty level. After Katrina, many made a mass exodus, leaving behind a city destroyed and forgotten. It seems that other cities got the funds for Mississippi, but certainly not Gulfport. Although I got an awesome deal on a property, I could not even find anyone living there that could afford the $750 per month I was seeking for rent. Did I mention it was 3 bedrooms? Eventually, I had to continue to make reductions until I was able to rent it to a family (2 working adults) who was able to rent it for $450 per month. When one of them was laid off, they stopped paying. By the time I evicted them, they had trashed the place. Unwilling to throw anymore good money after bad money, I gave it back to the bank.

Although this was a terrible experience, because the property was so cheap to begin with, I really only took a loss for the amount of the down payment and closing costs—about $15,000 in total. And I was able to write that off. So imagine if I had made a huge investment instead? While my earning potential would be greater, my loss potential would have also been greater.

This is why I encourage you to not tie all your assets up into one investment, specifically an apartment building. Look at it this way: It is far better to have 10 small properties that each net you $500 a month, than one large property that nets you $5,000 per month. In the first scenario, you can spread your risk out very thinly over multiple properties in multiple markets. So if one market crashes, then another market might be doing well. Also, you have more flexibility if you might need to pull cash out of one or two without affecting the others.

You should also diversify your investments as well. It's good to have at least one 401(k).

Step 4: Don't Cross-Collateralize

Cross-Collateralization is an investment strategy of using the equity in one property to secure the loan of a second property. Another application of this investment strategy is to use the earnings of one property to offset the losses of a second property for the purpose of securing a loan. Any application of this investment strategy is a bad idea for several reasons:

- A. You lose control over both properties. You will need permission from the lender in order to refinance, sell or make major changes or improvements. This can't work. You need to maintain control of your assets. You need to have the flexibility to refinance or sell, or to take any steps you deem necessary to execute your business plan without getting permission from some lender.

- B. You put both properties at risk. If things take a turn for the worst, and you find yourself in a position of losing a property; if they are cross-collateralized, you will lose both, even if one is still profitable.

Just remember, cross-collateralization is bad news for the borrower. Avoid it at all costs.

11

FREEDOM KEY #10

A PENNY SAVED IS A PENNY EARNED

We talked in an earlier chapter about being good stewards. Being frugal is a huge part of that good stewardship. Now notice I said frugal, not cheap—there is a difference. Being cheap brings about miserly thoughts of some stingy Scrooge clinching and hoarding their money as if someone is lurking around the bend to take it. Being frugal is not that at all.

A person that is frugal is savvy in their role as a steward of God's treasure. They take this responsibility of stewardship very seriously. They are shrewd in striking the best deal for all expenditures. Frugality does not indicate stinginess or hoarding traits, but rather, indicates generosity to those in need, as led by the Holy Spirit.

A cheap person may leave their server a $1 tip on a $40 check after enjoying wonderful service. A frugal person would never slight a hard-working person in this way; he would leave a 15% to 20% tip.

A frugal person is a shrewd negotiator. They understand that everything is negotiable. This frugal person recognizes that their business is important to merchants; and accordingly, marks their calendar for contract renewal dates of all subscription services; and negotiates for better rates.

If you haven't guessed by now, I am a frugal person. God had a good laugh when he put me together with my husband, who is my opposite in this area. Our biggest disagreements often occur in the grocery store. My husband goes to the grocery store and buys whatever he wants. He doesn't look at prices; he just gets what he wants. If he wants to buy a box of macaroni noodles, he will just grab one, usually the name brand, and toss it in the basket. On the other hand, I will see which brand is on sale, or ultimately the least expensive. I mean, what's the difference between the brand name macaroni noodle and the store brand one?

Inevitably, the cart will be filled with stupid stuff, like some gourmet cheese spread that he is going to try once, realize it's nasty and then leave in the refrigerator to rot. I will pick up an item in the cart that he has tossed in, and I will ask, "How much did this cost?" He will immediately blurt out, "$1.47" or some other random, small amount. And in this moment, I know God is having himself a good laugh at the two of us in the grocery store. I have just learned to shake my head and enjoy the laugh along with God.

I have listed a few tips that may be helpful in your quest to becoming frugal:

Tip Number 1: Refinance

Refinance your mortgage for a better rate. Ask your existing mortgage holder first. Tell them you want a better rate. Negotiate with them to waive your closing costs and fees. Some banks will do it; it's worth a try. If they waive the fees, you are saving as much as $10,000 of your valuable equity. By refinancing, you could experience some pretty substantial savings. Here is an example of what you could save by refinancing:

The family in this example has a $200,000 mortgage with a 30-year fixed rate of 6.5%. If they refinance at 4.5%, they will save about $2,400 per year on their monthly mortgage payment, and over $80,000 in interest charges over the life of the loan. They will have to use about $7,000 of their equity for refinancing costs, but as you can see, they easily recoup their costs in less than two years.

Whatever savings you experience from your reduced mortgage should be saved. Do not increase your expenses by the amount of your savings.

Tip Number 2: Auto Loan Bailout

If you have already made the mistake of financing a car, <u>as a one-time bailout</u>, refinance your mortgage and pull cash out to pay off that loan. This transfers that bad debt into good debt. Let me explain:

If the person in this example has a $30,000 car loan with a $750 per month payment, this is just money being spent with no benefit, other than the use of the car. If this person refinances their home and pulls out $30,000, then pays off the car, then:

A. The mortgage payment will increase only by about $125 after the refinance; and the $750 car payment will be eliminated.

B. The $30,000 debt now switches over from being bad debt (installment loan) and now becomes good debt (tax deductible mortgage interest).

C. The person does not lose the benefit of the use of the car.

I have some stern warnings about doing this, though:

This needs to be a one-time thing to bail you out of a bad situation. You cannot make a habit of using your equity in your home to resolve bad debt and poor spending decisions.

Once you bail yourself out, vow to never buy a car with a loan again.

Take whatever savings you have from this refinance, and put it directly into an account. This will be the funds you will use to purchase your next vehicle.

In this example, this family will have an extra $625 in their budget. This will allow them to save $7,500 per year. In 3 years, they would have saved $25,000, which could be:

    A. Used to purchase an investment property;

    B. Used to boost a college fund or other long-term growth vehicle; or

    C. Used to purchase a very nice pre-owned car without payment.

This savings could also just be set aside for emergency funds. It just cannot be used to increase monthly spending or to purchase other depreciating assets, such as TVs and electronics.

Tip Number 3 - Everything Is Negotiable

Remember, everything is negotiable. Regularly renegotiate your paid monthly services. Your cell phone bills, cable bill, satellite radio bill, everything. Here's how to do it: Call the provider and tell them you wish to cancel your service. They will automatically send you to their retention department. There, they are authorized to offer you discounts to convince you to stay with them. Arm yourself with some competitors' ads so you can use that information to garner a better reduction. Then set an alarm on your phone for when this offer will be expiring. As soon as it expires, do the same thing again. Do this for every service you are using.

Tip Number 4 - Buy Gym Memberships at Discount Warehouses

Gym membership discounts can be found at Costco and Sam's. They sell the type of memberships that you buy in advance. They sell a 2 or 3-year membership for a discounted price. For example, if you buy the membership at the gym, the price might be $30 per month x 12 months totaling about $360; whereas, Costco might offer a 2-year membership for $350. So you basically get the membership for half price.

12

CONCLUSION

So. The keys to the kingdom are in your hands. Now what will you do with them? They are useless unless you put them to work immediately.

Overcome any feelings you may be having of being overwhelmed with the idea of changing your life all at once, just start. Implement just one of the principles immediately. This will energize you and help you to gain confidence in your ability to achieve financial freedom. You can do it! Remember, financial freedom is available to anyone who is willing to follow the steps outlined in this book. You don't need to earn a huge salary, have advanced degrees, or have special gifts or talents. These are common sense steps and skills that anyone can master.

Anticipate and combat useless thoughts of fear. Human nature causes us to fear change. Part of it is our fear that we might have to give up something, or our fear of failing, but mostly we fear that this change will leave us in a worse position. But if you learned you had inherited a fortune, would you fear those changes that would come along with that? Likely not, because it is fairly certain that unless you are foolish, the change would leave you in a better position. Approach the steps in this process much the same as you would approach the life changes that would come along with inheriting a fortune – fully confident that the life changes you implement will leave you in a much better position.

Anticipate and combat opposition from The Enemy in all forms. Even discouragement from well-meaning loved ones. Only share your plans with people you are certain will support and encourage you. Keep moving forward, focused on your ultimate goals.

But most importantly, JUST START!

So let's look again at these ten keys. I want a promise from you that before you get up from reading this book, you will identify at least one of these 10 Keys that you can immediately implement.

10 Keys to Financial Freedom At An Early Age

1. Honor God with your firstfruits.
   Give back to God the first 10% of all your earnings.
   Give God the first of any new financial blessings.

2. Live below your means.
   Track your income and expenses.
   Know the difference between bad debt
      and good debt.

3, Submit yourself to a strict budget.
   Learn to live on no more than 70%
      of your earnings.
   Give the first 10% to God.
   Pay yourself next with 10% to savings.
   Put 10% into your investment fund.

4. Set financial goals.
   Set monthly goals, annual goals, and
      long-term goals.
   Cultivate your garden.

5. Master effective time management.
   Work from lists every day.
   Utilize Stephen Covey's 4-quadrant time
      management tool.

6. Resist lifestyle inflation.
   As income increases, do not increase
      expenses accordingly.
   Save raises and bonuses.

7. Be grateful and content.
   Be grateful for everything.
   Learn to be happy with what you have.

8. Master delayed gratification.
   Delayed gratification is the ability to resist the impulse to take an immediately available reward, in the hopes of obtaining a more valued reward in the future.

9. Real Estate is the best investment for building wealth.
   Invest in condos.
   Start small.
   Diversify your investments.
   Don't cross collateralize.

10. Be frugal.
    Refinance your mortgage for a better interest rate.
    Refinance your auto loan—one-time bailout.
    Re-negotiate all monthly subscriptions.
    Buy gym memberships at discount warehouses.

So, pick at least one of these keys that you will implement immediately – not next week, but right now.

I believe nothing happens that God does not use to better prepare you for the great works to which He has called you. However this little book got into your hands today, trust me, it was no accident.

I pray you will find much success on your journey.

www.ingramcontent.com/pod-product-compliance
Lightning Source LLC
Chambersburg PA
CBHW070105210526
45170CB00013B/750